MY THOUGHTS

SANDRIYA DCRUZ

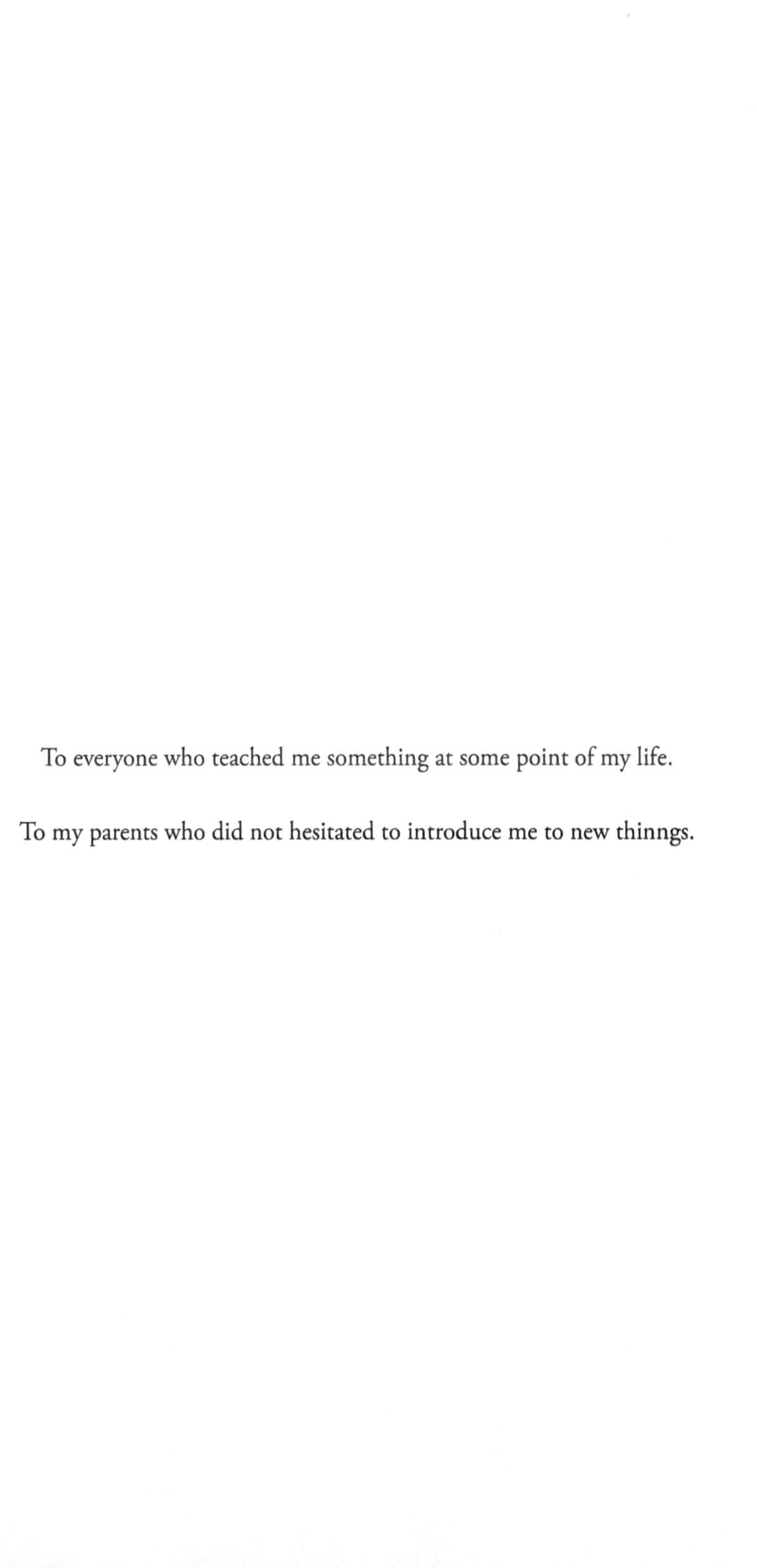

To everyone who teached me something at some point of my life.

To my parents who did not hesitated to introduce me to new thinngs.

Contents

Preface

When i was 7 year old i wondered how things worked. I was curious to know why my parents kept on saying "world is cruel, be strong enough to bear things. NO one is going to treat you like us".

my innocense, thought that everyone is kind and genuine but as i grew up i realized, how wrong my thinking was and how right were my parents.

as i obsereved people in love, cruelty in world, Different feeling, different people

i finally thought to write about it.

from my prespective.

POEMS in this book are not connected to eachother but are somehow connected to our lives

- SANDRIYA DCRUZ

1. LIFE I HAD

my windows wide-opened
welcomed the breeze of heat,
my mind opened on the shore of the sea.
What time is it, I have no clue
I am old and my thoughts are coming out of the blue.
My body cannot allow me to surf on waves
'oh' I miss when life was young and I was brave.
Shell collected by me got lost in the length of the sea
I wanted it to last with me but the door was locked with no keys.
Only if I knew this would be near
Where my life would be working with no gear
Hoping to experience what I lost no matter what's the cost.

2. JUNE

The warm summer breeze
Mocktail adorned with berries and fresh mint leaves
Oh! Vacation captured my heart
Love and joy in abundance
The final words spoken without regret
All was invaluable
The moments
the people
all invaluable
Love and emotions overflowing
Each time felt like the first
The azure ocean
Mirroring the sky above
As I delved deeper
disconnecting from the world
June
the magician of life
Unveiling hidden feelings
Love, once lost
All now feels fresh and new
The month of love
The month of joy
Life feels alive and fresh
All is well

Our minds at ease
Days unfold lazily
No stress, just freedom
Do as you please
Life in harmony
Capturing moments
To take away with me
Reading book while siting under a tree

3. THE SAVIOUR

4. DREAMY

We can't focus on ourselves when we are stressed from the mess
"life is short do hard"
Fed up of the words, even from the world
Going in the dark, looking at the moon and stars
Considering I'll be one of them if I don't work
Society with ugly scars Won't understand
For them strangers ashes are as same as a beach sand
Days passed
Still here we are
In the crowd facing everyone just like us
Probably manifesting to get hit by a bus
long days with endless work is nightmare of all teens
tough grind
wise mind
would be required to get out of this trash bin

5. CRUEL WORLD

The cost of life here is high to achieve

Three truths I am wiser to understand

Endless labour, lack of love, and solitude to confront

Each of us here is crafting our destiny

The calm of death will elude all

For the sake of profit, some may even harm their loved ones

The cycle of life persists, even if beliefs are tested.

One's rights can be taken by those with deceitful intentions

The reality of the situation remains concealed

The cosmos is the cause

Homes lie in ruins

Lives are stolen

Leaders of the nation are preoccupied with pursuing glory and power

Love is merely a facade, all appear self-centered here

And the sufferers bear the brunt.

Four lessons to grasp

Be cautious, forgive yet do not forget, love and show respect, but guard your vulnerabilities

The world is harsh beyond imagination

Fear, mistakes more than earthworms

6. INSOMNIA

Sleeping at night is not my thing
I dwell in the dark.
Maybe there will be waiting something for me with a spark.
Restless days, longing for peace
Perhaps that's the reason I cannot sleep.
Failing in every single word I speak
That does not bother me, because there is no one to peep.
Every single confession I make stays in dark and fades away.
Every night, I can feel my heart fall apart from the memory of past
And then again in the morning routine starts.

7. LUST

My eyes were closed by the hands of the unknown.
Soul of mine was drained breaking thousands of my bones.
Sweat became blood flowing from every inch of my skin
a Scream of mine disappeared within the dark
Filing the silence with dogs' bark.
All my ears were left to hear was men's lust over my figure
Filling my mouth with ugly liquor.
My eyes shattered, my soul went high
Watching from above, dead me someone would find
As Time passed my body decayed
No one came
and just like me thousands of bodies were strayed

8. SORROW

I become the situation with heat
I am inside every one of the different breeds.
I make smiley faces cry with tears
Old men swallow me with a gulp of beer.
Only if I had the power to control
I would choose how to react and how much more.
I am just a word with thousands of kinds
I make the day of a person
Men explain me to their female version.
Sometimes they hide me within them
Some noble people write about me with a pen.

9. SUICIDE

I became the throne of my rose
Ended my own life with thousands of goals.
My cup got full of dirt
nothing was left to insert.
Funny how I left everyone behind
It was ironic how no one was mine
Words of mine were left in a slot
While my ashes were being filled in a pot

10. DAD

In shadows hiding memories deep,
A daughter's heart, where hunger for love was keep.
A longing glance, a fleeting smile,
Yearning for attention across the miles.
Daddy's girl, but the distance grows,
Emotions tangled, where sorrow flows.
In childhood dreams, a hero's embrace,
Now fractured echoes, without a trace.
A father's love, a pillar on wall
Yet cracks appear, like a fragile wall.
Unspoken words, wounds left unseen,
In the silence, where pain has been.
Seeking solace in another's arms,
Trying to fill the void with false alarms.
But ghosts of the past, they linger still,
A haunting presence, a void to fill.
Yearning for approval, for words of pride,
But silence echoes, on the other side.
Daddy issues, a heavy burden to bear,
In the heart's depths, a silent prayer.
Yet strength emerges from within,
A daughter's journey to begin.
To heal the wounds, to find her way,
Beyond the shadows of yesterday.

For love exists in many forms,
In gentle hearts and quiet storms.
Though daddy's issues leave their mark,
A daughter's light can still embark.
To rewrite the tale, to break the chain,
To find her voice amidst the pain.
For in the journey, she'll come to see,
Her worth defined her spirit free.

11. UNKNOWN ME

I forgot who I was
once I entered a group of disguises.
Droll how everyone tried to fit in
Thinking they are cool while committing sin.
Just like them stupid me went with the flow of Poseur
Just to get some public disclosure.
The whole filled my mind
How foolish I seemed once everything was over and I realized I was blind.

12. UNKNOWN FAMILY

That night everything ended in a cold breeze
When my family left me under a tree.
The way I was loved by everyone, I never knew I would be in this stream
Where all I would want is for my soul to be freed.
Growing up without made me occupied yet alone
the Reason for them leaving me is just so unknown
Are they dead, or alive? I don't know, I don't want to know.*
Laying on my deathbed hoping someone would come
Maybe a glimpse of my mother from heaven will shine
Noting appears and my eyes go blind

13. UNKNOW PEOPLE

Some people are just given a glance over
No one knows about their past
Their present is unknown
All they feel like is a leftover
You don't feel scared when they are around
All you feel is the curiosity rushing through your veins.
"We don't know anything about their pain"
"What's their motive?"
Is so unknown
Town and cities old and frown
They belong there
For cold nature as if they are carrying a crown
Or maybe it's their nature
Like us
Some are happy
Some are sappy
Some are serious
Some are immature
And some are mysterious
From person to person, lives to lives
All of us are distinguished from each other
And some are just unknown
You capture them once
And they fill your mind with themselves

MY THOUGHTS

Uttering many questions in mind
Who they are?
And why the answer to my query
Is just so far

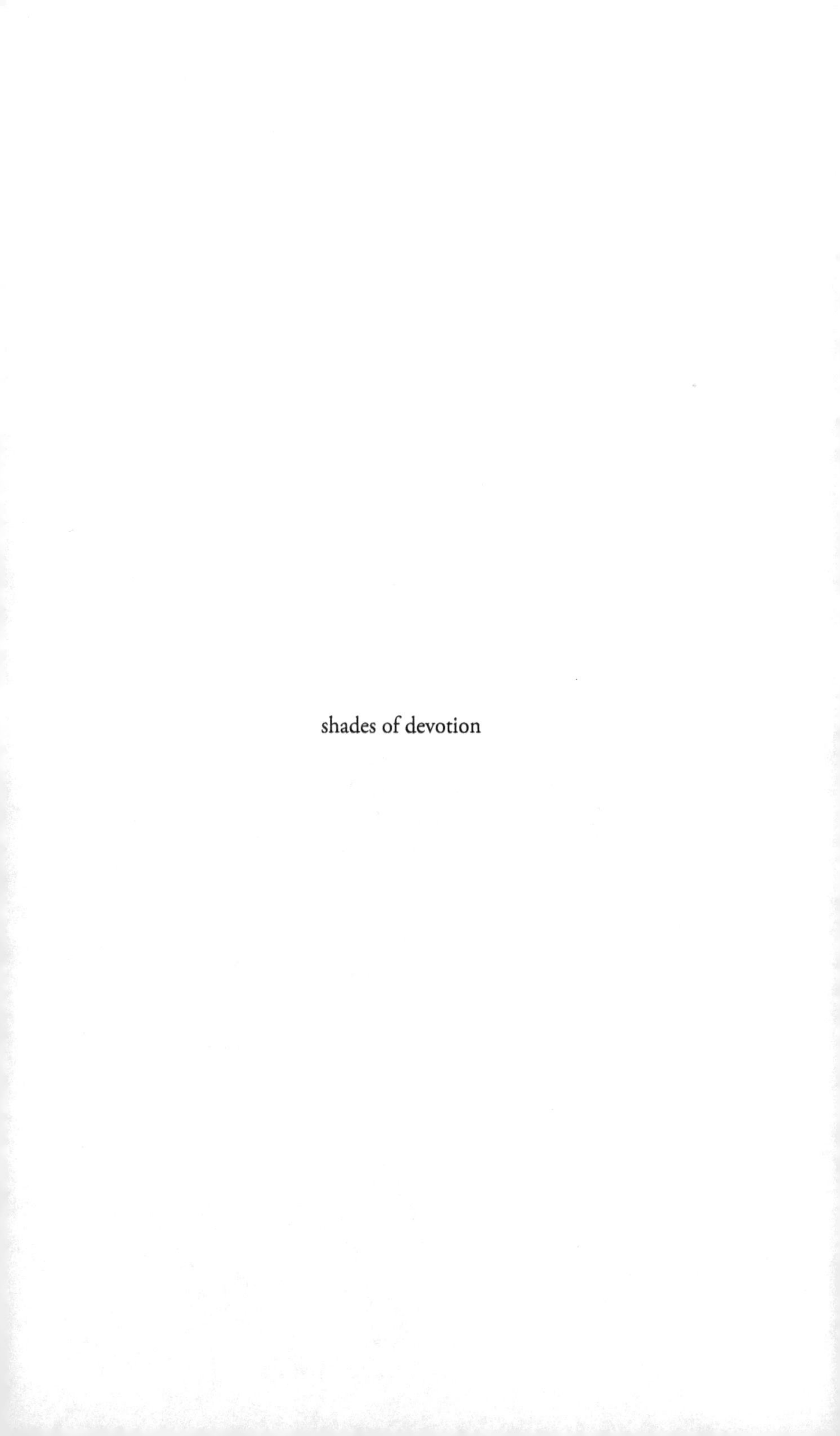

shades of devotion

14. HIM

She was a rainbow, yet he was blind to colors.

His appearance was a gem, but his heart remained shallow within.

Perhaps the suffering he endured left him numb.

His allure never returned. With time, he descended deeper.

Enduring much, he uttered not a word. Struggling to exist in this realm.

All she could offer was her prayers, yet his life did not conclude well.

15. LOVE

Painters care towards a painting they made
Care of parents for their child, who they made
A pet owners love towards their pet.
Love takes on various forms,
Children adore cartoons in swarm,
Youngsters fancy bikes in dorms,
Love remains a unifying norm.
Love isn't bound by status or label,
Whether in marriage or courtship stable,
In each other, finding solace substantial,
Love shines bright, life's precious fable.
In love's essence, greatness beheld,
Bringing joy to some, for others it may weld,
A spectrum vast, tales so oft compelled.

16. first and last

You were my first and final to be embraced and sensed

All those that came after you were both

Foe and friend

Oh, my beloved

I tarnished our connection

My heart aches upon seeing your reflection

I pass by your home just to glimpse at you

At times, I am fortunate enough to peer into those affection-filled brown

eyes

Perhaps our past

caused the fractures

hopefully the future reunites us

every endeavour I undertook to win you over

I beseech God that it doesn't go in vain

To obtain what I had

It's just you and me

Every memory of our time together remains intact

17. ONE SIDED ME

it's puzzling how you intertwined yourself with mine
You cross my mind each time,
I can't help but find
Afraid to admit
, fearing our bond will unwind
Once more
hesitant to inquire, your desires undefined
What if I fail, hence I write it on sheet in a line
How do I perceive what you define
Longing to borrow your essence for a while
To grasp your sentiments, to reconcile
Uncertain if redemption will compile
I gather my expectations all the while
Inscribed my trust in you, in every message i compile

18. CULPRIT

You can split my heart in two
After it mends, it still beats for you.
Being hollow
Is much easier than feeling love
Almost obsessed with you
With my dreams soaring above.
Can I have you back once more?
To experience what I have in store.
You are the bloom of my days that withered
Yet still present in my thoughts.
Your wilted petals hold my gaze.
Why did you leave and where

19. TOXIC RELATIONSHIP

He was like an umbrella carried by me in the storm,
just hit me once and my whole life fell into a gloom
I never knew he would be that dangerous.
until I saw his core.
too afraid to show him the mirror,
I knew he would just call me a whore.
My respect flowed in an endless river
which broke my own heart and made my body shiver.
Astonished by how such a person can be a part of my desire.
Remembering that's not what he showed himself when we first met.
someone who tore me apart, but with whom I still have to share my bed.

20. DEJA VU

You remind me of someone I never met
Talk walk moments we spent together rewind
Yet I cannot recall when I claimed you as mine.
The face, the eyes, the lips, I have never seen but seen
Maybe I was in my dreams where you came into the scene.
You made it all look like I was in my fifteen again.
When, how, and where never indicated
Because you were just unrequited
I hope to meet you in my actual life
Where we are reunited.

21. BOOKS

In pages worn by countless hands,
Lies a world where wonder stands.
Each word a whisper, each sentence a song,
A tapestry of tales, where hearts belong.
Love for books, a timeless art,
Binding minds and souls apart.
From dusty shelves to cozy nooks,
A sanctuary found in books.
In every chapter, a new friend,
Where journeys start and dreams extend.
From fantasy realms to histories old,
Stories untold, yet boldly told.
In ink-stained lines, emotions flow,
The thrill of mystery, the depth of woe.
Through poetry's rhyme, and prose's grace,
Books embrace, in every space.
They teach, they challenge, they ignite,
Imagination's endless flight.
In silent hours, they speak profound,
In whispers soft, without a sound.
Love for books, a sacred bond,
Where minds and hearts respond.
For in their pages, we explore,
The depths of human thought and more.

So let us cherish, and let us read,
For books fulfill our deepest need.
In love for books, our spirits soar,
Forever rich, forever more.

22. WHY

In the dance of lies, he took his chance,
A cheater boy with a reckless stance.
Charming smiles hid deceitful eyes,
Promises woven with silky lies.
He whispered love, like a soothing song,
Yet deceit lingered all along.
In the shadows, secrets he kept,
While hearts in innocence, they wept.
A master of words, a player's game,
He played with hearts, without shame.
Each embrace a web, each kiss a snare,
Leaving behind hearts in despair.
He craved the thrill of stolen bliss,
Unaware of the hurt he'd dismiss.
Fleeting moments, empty and cold,
A cheater boy, his story told.
But hearts mend, though scars remain,
Lessons learned through tears and pain.
For cheater boys may come and go,
But true love's light will always glow.
So beware the cheater boy's allure,
His fleeting charm, his love impure.
In the end, it's honesty that prevails,
In hearts that mend and love that sails.

THANKYOU READER

for reading my poems hope you liked them

the chapters are limited i know but if the response would be satisfactory

i would defenietly realeas a part 2

if you have any suggestions or query, you email me on my gmail Id

(dcruzsandriya@gmail.com)

i post some of my poetry on my instagram handle

(sandriya_dcruz)

-sandriya

www.ingramcontent.com/pod-product-compliance
Lightning Source LLC
Chambersburg PA
CBHW021154130726
47988CB00004B/1600